THE BLACK MARKS HE MADE

THE
BLACK
MARKS
HE MADE

Poetry By

SHOTSIE GORMAN

NEW YORK

Printed and Published
in the
United States by
PROTEUS PRESS, INC.
Albany, New York

NEW YORK

The Black Marks He Made
First Edition
Shotsie Gorman

Book design by Cynthia DeMichele
Production by Associated Creative Services, Inc.

Hardcover ISBN 0-9631708-5-6
Softcover ISBN 0-9631708-6-4

INTRODUCTION

Let me pull on your coat about something. If you were sitting in an audience now, I could see your eyes; I'd know that you were feeling our connection. I would take the time to tell you something of the inspiration — something of the poetry's source. If I had your eyes though, I know I would try to get you to laugh first. This would be my way to relieve you before I started pushing the emotional envelope. I would do my best to verbally create expectations for the next poem, setting up one level of comfort then shape-shifting into the darker places. It's true, I would prefer to see you, but I am very grateful for your eyes on the page now.

If I am a stranger to you, I have to let you in on the fact that for the last twenty two years I have been mostly focusing on being a Professional Tattoo Artist. I have spent much of my waking time marking people with images that inscribe their deepest fears and greatest aspirations for all to see. By tracing many a black mark on their skins I have been drawn into an odyssey of sorts that has transformed my consciousness. The marks I've created became a map directing my life's path. Tattooing has come to clearly represent my first step in a long walk into a deep spiritual healing process. Poets are often seen as misfits, queers, eccentrics and outsiders. Keep in mind that tattooists also fall into the latter categories.

There is a clearly a pervasive fear of basic human emotions that dominates our American landscape. It has, in my view, greatly contributed to the recent rash of adolescent acts of remorseless violence. The denial of our emotional needs has directly damaged structural foundation of human interactions. Making us a people without compassion. No doubt this void that is growing between heart, body, mind and its clash with our fundamentally essential need to hear brutal emotional truths, passionate sensual, and sexual expressions of love are the major impetus for young people, and for that matter, many people to be so urgently drawn to both forms of my expression — tattooing and poetry.

continued

I came to tattooing, in retrospect, to learn to lose my fear of intimacy. This legacy of personal healing I owe to my clients over the years. They have taught me to lose my judgments, to embrace all this suffering and joy of life as tools for healing. It was the tattoo saga and my Paterson experience that set free my poetic voice. I became more open and inspired by the likes of Allen Ginsberg, for his courage to express the darkest of his desires in an honest way, Amiri Baraka for his freedom fighter spirit, powerful sense of his heritage and musical connections, Hayden Carruth for his intellectually incisive language used to create clarity, Jimmy Santiago Baca's passion and pain, Rumie for his ecstatic revelations, telling hidden truths of his life's spiritual experience. By attending poetry readings and watching many talented people stand up and speak the harsh truths and sublime visions of their lives, moving all of us as one spirit from joy to tears, has energized the spark in my creative life to speak out in a blazing fire.

A butterfly
even when pursued,
never seems to
be in a hurry.

It struck me while trying to capture the words like Buson's butterflies, that ambiguity, while the very foundation of the visual forms of expression can be a plague to the poet. I've tried to cut to the chase if you will, with my poetry recounting the voices of Paterson. I was inspired, more, driven to put many of them to rest, knowing that once their wings were touched they would not fly again until you bring your eyes and heart to them. Through tattooing and poetry I have brought much emotional clarity home, to my heart.

When I began writing this series of reminiscences of coming up in Paterson, I had the intention to write short stories about my cast of wacky friends and experiences. Although "We all start out with bad direction," to quote Tom Waits, what began to emerge within those considerations were portraits of my old friends from the Brook Sloate Housing Projects, dominated by their fathers. The fathers loomed large physically, and as the impetus for our later actions. They began to speak out to me of their loneliness, fears, and sufferings, unraveling their legacies like string on frayed cuffs, followed as markers for the way home by their sons.

The poets' truth — truth of an emotional type — stands mostly unspoken between father and sons. It seems clear to me, as a result the struggle we face as men is primarily to maintain a decent level of open communication between ourselves and other male friends. Unfortunately there generally has to be a high level of ritual, or humor, as the stage for any real connection. This debilitating circumstance is what I attempt to address in many of my poems. Through writing I've exorcised many shadows placed deep in my soul by a bright lack of emotional intimacy between myself and the significant men in my life; i.e. Grandfather, Uncle, and Father — as well as the lack of such connections later in life. Making "Black Marks" has stitched closed many "bloody rips in my own family circle." I did so, in hindsight, for the sake of my children, and with a desire to live a fruitful life, whole cloth as a fully awake human being.

Despite the surprised looks I receive both from the tattoo crowd when I say poetry, and the poetry folks I encounter in my role as tattooist, I have found that they, upon their reading my work or hearing me perform, understand tattooing and poetry are not strangers. In the end, "we" are all of the same family.

Shotsie

For My Family...

Dvo Faciem Idem
Non Est Idem

Two may have the same idea
and it is not the same idea.

TABLE OF CONTENTS

continued

TABLE OF CONTENTS (continued)

THE BLACK MARKS HE MADE

WINGERS

Somebody winged that cigarette;
It seemed to fall from the sky.
Red sparks shot all around where it landed.
Long after the car whizzed by,
seemed like, with
Gene-Ammons-playing-that-tone-like-Debra-Winger's
voice I heard, and dammmm!
she-is-hot-like-licks-from-Bird.

VOTING BOOTH QUICKIE

Today, I am supposed to swell with civic pride
but I just feel small and dirty.
The voting booths sat like fat, middle-aged,
institutionalized, mental patients with their mouths open
Squatting on all four sides of the town meeting hall.

The League of Women Voter ladies, pissed, because they'd
found an S name listed in the A-to-G book,
sniped at one another like drivers on the Jersey Turnpike.
I am shocked to realize
that the color that dominates this farce
is exactly the same as in the police interrogation room
I saw in nineteen sixty-eight,
when I witnessed cops
beat my black friend Billy Crawley.
His blood looked so dark against the government green;
Even the blood of the world at large
looks so dark against our green.

I nervously noted a blue-haired woman was stitching
my white voting coupon onto a green length of string.
The pile looked like so many grounded kites.
The polyester curtains reminded me of the Royal Motel
on Route Three in Secaucus, New Jersey,
Where you can get a room for
three hours for twenty bucks.

When the lever slammed down I felt shame;
I was relieved when I turned to see
the seam in the crumpled curtain was sealed.
My actions would be covered.
I came out feeling the same lack of satisfaction
that a virgin losing his virginity
to a ten dollar whore would,
humiliated by the voting booth quickie.

WORKIN, HE BE WORKIN

Dim visions and fat

Why would a workin man care what Ivana Trump be wearin?

Why does he sit listening to Bob Grant and by him be swearin?

When he needs protection, he be callin his union,

then, why he want to be with Republicans, Newtswoonin?

Do a fat white man identify with Rush, to his death?

Even though he never sat at a desk, or had an easy takin breath

do he say "welfare" while his face is a-snearin,

because he mean Blacks n' Latinos taken his place, he be fearin?

Do he think that?

YOU DON'T NEED REFERENCES
TO BORROW TROUBLE

Wasn't till the matriarch,
Clara's death bed,
she admitted.
Wasn't till Joseph the patriarch's
death bed he accused her.

While Tom,
Clara's husband of 45 years,
could do no more
than Alzheimer shake.
Mouths gaped, at the news uttered by Clara
that Vernon, standing in worn brown shoes,
was not her younger brother
but in reality her son.
They all watched in the stunned silence
as the orderly washed the floor of the room.

Life wasn't at all
what everyone thought it was.
Nor what it would be.
Vernon shuddered, thinking
how he always understood himself as Clara's
bastard child of incestuous rape
as the heat rose through his eyes

Bastard child
of grandfather rape.
Wasn't true.
He repeated, to the rhythm
of the heart monitor's beep.
Flashing an amber
diagram of mother heart mountains
across the dark screen.
Almost unheard
over the thunder of his.
48 years of
guilt and fear solar flared in front of him.
Sweating over his children being deformed

He watched his life pass before him
in the clear dripping IV.
Attached
to his mother.
After all
he did expect his mother
to finally admit
he
was really her son
at last.
But the razor truth
that his grandfather was not his father,
Flushed him like the umbilical
morphine drip
warmed his mother.

Vernon trembled.
His large Adam's apple rising and falling
Like the respirator plunger,
pumping pressure of truth
through expanded temporal arteries.
Vernon stumbled forward;
numbness like blood-soaked wool
enclosed him.
Again.
Again.
Same as when
he was a boy and watched
Joseph and Clara
grope each other
in a dark coffin-filled room.

Beads of liquid,
that tasted of salt blood,
pricked by the crown of life,
poured down his face.
Into the corners of his mouth
that remained open.
The white phone rang
while
Tom
Alzheimer
shook.

HALE BOP SHOO BOP

"Hey man, did ya see it?"

"What?"

"Haley Bop?"

"You mean Bill Haley?"

"No, man, the comet!"

"Yeah! Bill Haley and the Comets.

Dig the millennium dude."

Hale Bop—Shoo-Bop!

"Come on! I'm serious man, they believed an alien spaceship come
to take them was trailing in the tail of the comet."

"Yeah, but did they believe a guy who died and came back to life
and now lives in the sky?"

"Huh?"

Bop shoo haley bop bop

"In the tail, man, the tail of the comet —
I read somewhere that it's 287 million miles long,
datsa lotta tail man, ahuh and those wackos actually put their
faith in getting on board a spaceship after death."

"You mean they had faith?"

Bop shoo bop!

"Whadja mean, about the guy comin back after death, Hanh?
Did those weirdoes believe in a guy dyin and coming back to life.
Whoa, like an alien man, no maybe like a zombie."
"No, the zombies were busy watching TV."

Bop shoo bop hale

Do waaa do waaa

"Do you really think anyone actually buys it?"

"Whadaya mean? The Heaven's Gate cult, the Pearly Gate to Heaven cult or whatever it was called?"

"No man, the self-inflicted delusions, the self-flagellating set of boundaries that deny the truth of existence. I mean... do the hard assed followers of the word, the rules, that refuse to see living life and sex are the true gifts and there's no bullshit prize in the end, ones that fear their own death and actually take myths that defy everyone's real life experience and accept them as hard historical facts, while denying the power of thought that we are all of the same divine energy and can't love. The ones who so easily kill off any who would deny them of control."

"Huh?"

Do waaa do waaa do ya?

Bop shoo bop!

Censorship

DARK BRANCHES

We were running scared
like deer
through the buffalo grass.
The smell of its seeds flying
filling us
while chasing down the screaming rabbit.

"Go ahead, do it!" Bleated out of me
the blood of our eyes
blotted out the blue sky.
Kenny raised the small hatchet over him.

"Kill 'em!
He's suffering!"

Small hind legs rushing under him
couldn't carry him away.
Like us he ran with all he had
and still could
not escape his pain.

The arrow pierced
his rear haunches
caught up in the low briar
held him fixed
Like the anger of our fathers
held us.

I ran up to our small St. Sebastian.
Took the hatchet into my hand
with raised arm, cursing in my father's voice
I struck the first blow
and caved in his head.
It ended his suffering,
I said. It was more of a question
in the voice of Brutus
I closed off his pain.

I thought.
I could do it for him
but not for us.

The second blow
was out of my jealousy
over his release
from this life.
The crunching
in dead grass
snapped closed my
feelings
for years.

JOE WILLIAMS ME

Say you need me, baby!
Say you need me, baby!
Say you need me in the night!

He projected, interjected, and suspected as much.
As much open-hearted energy as any man
could, in this time and place, clutch.

His eyes snapped inward.

Not the furtive glance,
no — not the long hard look
of a James-Baldwin-angry black man,
or the empty stare of a hungry man
out of the black,

but an endless eternal stare to the battleground within
without.

Say you need me, baby!
Say you need me, baby!
Say you need me in the night!
Shout it out!

You can't take away a man's drum!
He'll beat down on the trash cans,
and the seats of public toilets!
Max Roach me.
He'll beat on himself
Coltrane me
his music is sadly joyous.

Sa Sa Saxa
Saxa phone me!
Don't call me too late.

They was just now becoming aware of how obvious
the rumble in the streets of their souls
were to the tourists in their lives.
They burn it down with sounds that move too deep.
Ornette me.

Say you need me, baby!
Say you need me, baby!
Say you need me in the night!

Realizing the practice
of non-violence must now extend to self.
Knowing without a doubt there is
in the beat of a heart, a spiraling galaxy of sparkling souls,
a Hugh Masakela rhythm of eternity.

I have ta ask
Can you revel in the regularity?
Can you dance the watusi to mediocrity?
Can you hang on the four four beat
unchanged?
Can you dig the beat of the banal?

Joe Williams me!

Say you need me, baby!
Say you need me, baby!
Say you need me
in the night!

MIND IF I, SAY I?

"Mind if I nosy up and look at your painting?"
her voice hummed softly,
shimmering up my neck, the heat pelting.
"Yeah, sure," I said, Jersey deftly.

Almost blank paper seemed skeletal in arid space,
its whiteness a creative ether of Mojave spirits.
Pencil lines, more an embossing, in the sun erase.
Distilled moments struggle for merit.

Gazing up to her sound
there were sun-whipped white wisps of hair,
forming wavy, purple wheat marks on the ground.
No signs of distress on her face soft, fair.

Colorless silk blouse, small lace patterns
on the edge of scalloped collar cling.
her discerning eyes, deep-glinting cisterns
without the common circles of long-aged suffering.

"Will that be a painting?"
I smiled back. "Yes if I don't bake first."
Her hand swung in a small arcing,
like those of her thin silver brows pursed.

"Well, you folks are dedicated.
I'm sure this heat won't stop you."
What did she mean, "you folks," something unsaid?
Was it my tattoo?

Jersey folks — too obvious.
Forty five-year-old male?
Ahh yes — "Artists," I comment, spuriously,
"It's true, we are dedicated — I'm just not sure to what."

AKIRA KUROSAWA DIED TODAY – No. 1

Akira-
-ran-
-today
carrying with him his-shadow.
They said; he was a-worrier.

Caused him to stroke
they said, it was
with the slash of light
he wrote.

Don't rush-a-man
it takes time
to speak.

AKIRA KUROSAWA DIED TODAY – No. 2

Akira died today while I sat,
fat-assed in my kitchen.
Stuffing my face with a French pastry.
Reading the local paper on how
yoga was becoming mainstream
because of Madonna.

When I heard it.
Droning out of the blue Japanese TV
Akira Kurosawa died today of heart failure.
Today?
Before I finished my swallow?

Before our paths crossed
in a world of shadows.
Before, I could drink my
Italian Cappuccino
tears rolled down.

My new friend Tom Woglom
Was star struck by Madonna who recently
sent flowers to Les Paul's hospital room
while Tom laid in the next bed after
open heart surgery.

Soaking up the tears
and the news that Yoga
was becoming mainstream.
I considered;
How would
America respond
to Akira's passing?
With seven flowers, or yoga?
It was a tough decision for us after all.
We're Americans.
Lets have some more Creme Brulée
and think about it.

HE WANTED NOTHING
AND LEFT NOTHING BUT WANTING

Like the animals he wagered on
he ran
around and around.
Always looking
for new emotional currency.

Spent them,
Mother, father,
friend,
sister, brother
wife
and daughter
one
by
one.

Each daily double
drove
the thundering hoof prints
of separation
deeper.

Locked down in his cell,
you have to wonder,
did he keep accounts
of this legacy of hurt,
he hoarded
in stay of
family,
house,
and home?

I'll
bet
he
did.

CONSTELLATION

(After Gerard Manley Hopkins)

The garrison
gun belt dropped
fully loaded to the kitchen table.
At the very instant my hand felt the
spring tension and weight of the
light switch snapping on.

Synchronicity
as it often does
startled me.
It was as if the light swelling this
small space had
knocked something loose there.

I first glanced up to the light fixture overhead.
It hung, a supple breast.
Bathing all in waves of milky light.
Curved
silk like the link from buttock to thigh.
The small embossed flowers
formed a lace panty pattern
ozone perfumed.

On approach the house was dark.
I slipped the key in the door deftly.
Weighting each moment with stealth.
Even so the light shot out loudly
on sharp angles at first.
Left to the kitchen.
Dotted chiaroscuro with small vignettes
of copper plates and dangling ivy on shelves.
Like a madman's mediocre vision
of domestic tranquility.

It shot right into the living room
passed the 12-inch black and white,
Lost in a faux blond wood salvation army box,
along with the victrola and
quarter, taped to the tone arm.

The light softened and rose
around the steel cornered plaster walls.
Vibrating at the same speed
as the chill of my spine,
As I made my way around
to survey the damage.

Standing in the dim light gun in hand
Pale light rolling up the cuffed blue
glinting off the badge and steel.

"Why the fuck are you so late!"
Sprung from the sparked shadow.

It's true, I thought.
Something did break there
in the kitchen.

SPOOKY

What I loved, really, was
my memory of him.
Francis, was my mother's youngest brother.
But reflecting now I realize
I knew Butch more by the artifacts of his life.

My feelings were almost archeological
After twenty years of separation
As the facts of his death were related to me —
by his sister sobbing
over a crackling phone connection.

"The prison lost his ashes in transit,"
missing the irony, she wept.
"It was UPS, she said, those bastards!"
bruised out on the static connection.

Butchy's ashes
to be dusted over the race track
like his life,
lost in transit.

Spooky, Casper the Ghost's comic,
bad boy other self —
was India ink etched into his right bicep.
First e mano by an old South Paterson Goombah
Who owed Butch a gambling debt.
Settled as he carved him a
Spooky tattoo.
Jabbed in by three sewing needles tied
together with thread
one poke at a time.

"Fuck you!" Butch said
each time,
keeping the rhythm
of-the-blood-beaded-jabs.

Spooky was to be sharpened
black and reshaped,
Its fedora cocked off-kilter
by me, in an attempt to revisit
our family connection.

Buzzing my heavy tattoo machines
in the dim light
of a sleazy Florida pool hall
and beer joint.
Listening to doo-wop.
Watching the blood drop.
I dreamed
in the still of that night
splashed with his red Neapolitan,
feverish with the knowledge
that it ran in my veins.
Slurred me to sleep
with tears for
his suffering.
Kneeling
before the image of him
Impaled on the x of his life.

And his faux tortoiseshell
hairbrush, left behind,
filled with strands of
brillcreamed black hair
and dandruff.
Sitting on his
highboy
blond dresser
with the loose change
of his life spilling out,
like an offering
below the spooky plaster Jesus head
with the concave eyes that followed
my every move.

STORE BOUGHT

"Do you want to take his teeth?"

"I think — I will —
Well, on second thought.
Leave 'em here in his bag."

"OK," she said, unclipping
the IV.

"See ya later Pop."

GRANDPA'S KITCHEN TRICKS

A drying Turkey wishbone dangled,
casting a gray shadow on the cracked blue walls.
Tied to the light's drop string,
along with a small grease-stained
yellow and white plastic pagoda,
that glowed in the dark
Like an Ed Wood prop.

"Come on-a my only grandson
make-a wish for papa to make-a-lottamoney
Pull the bone." He laughed.
Those long red peppers
strung together by a clot of brown string
hung over the chipped porcelain basin
made me sneeze, or I thought; it was because I had to rise up on
my toes to reach the handles
that triggered it.

He never pulled.
Holding onto his part of the Y shaped bone
with Pall Mall stained index and thumb.
His nail turning as red as my face
after a ritual rub with a coarse three day beard.

Although he pushed
roasted garlic onto hard, burnt bread.
He never pulled.
I'm not sure when it was I realized this.
The fat end of the Y
always ended up
on his end
of the
bone.

Maybe it was when he fought
with that brain tumor.
Trumpeted me in to watch my father shave him
in Saint Joseph's Hospital.

My father pulled
the razor over Grandpa's three day old beard
before
he rubbed me with it.
By then I knew;
just hold onto your end,
Just hold on.
Let all the others pull.

"Are they all here yet?"
"Yes Pa," my father choked out.
"Tell my boys to come in first, my grandson."
One by one they came
soaked, somber.
All the brothers
then my mother and all of her sisters.
Each having their say
stood in a Y at the foot of his bed.
"I go now." he said.
The fat end of the bone
in
his
hand.

HIGHWAY

In my mind's eye
I was speeding down the highway
to your heart
throbbing thighs.

250 pounds of turbo charged
red horse power
nostrils flared, flying fur.

There were no signs I could read
they were all a blur
speedometer melted under my gaze.

Trying to resist a
sense of the flashing
red light
in the rearview.

I could see an emotional
cop in it.
So I hit the brakes.
I swerved on the curve
of your thigh
I popped the parachute of my past
Slowed down the illusions
to a stall
and pulled over.

Still smoking in
the smoldering spin
I looked to my interior.
It was rolled
and pleated,
button-tufted
leather soft.
I pulled out my ID;
it spilled into the sky

turning it black and speckled
with pinholes of light.
It was so ebony
I could only see my face
in the pulse of the spinning
red rearview.

My artistic license intact
my present, squared chopped and channeled
a house, two kids on a small street, neat.

He leaned in through the open roof
"May I see proof of your wife sir?"
"Proof of my life sir?"
"No sir.
I saw you spin out on the curve
lost your self there
crossed the double line sir."

I handed him my present license
thinking I didn't want
to have him search my past
I included my poetry card.

He smiled and said,
"Slow down a bit sir.
You will get there soon enough
Watch out
don't turn for the guru sign
follow your own way
you'll be fine.
Have a good time sir."

Before I could ask
He was gone.
My eyes on the open
future highway gazed
I lit the way with
high powered quartz
halogen rhymes
Still warm from your
curves.

HER SMELL

Yes, yes of course, I miss her.
Her smell mostly,
when I travel.

This morning,
small flashes of bird shadows
passed over our bed;
cold, I wished for the rabbits
brown turning like
so many things unsaid —

I tried to tell if he was listening
when I said good-bye.
At six it's hard to know.
All he could think of was, snow.

In the window I saw mysterious
bulges and bumps made familiar
and seductive,
smoothed by white fallen winter.

Inside, the familiar bulges and curves
made mysterious by bunched blankets
and nuzzling cats for breasts.

Yeah, it was her smell
I clutched for
in the unfamiliar
bed of my travel,
her smell that I sucked in
with my first
morning breath
the day I left.

The sun was golden,
An orange yellow like the
egg yolks in Bologna.
What green there was
poked out through the snow.

In the colors I could almost smell
the pepper-and-egg sandwiches
my grandfather
would bring for lunch
to the silk mills.
I had to be in Paterson by 10,
when most of my youth
was spent trying to find
ways to get out.

A LOVER FOR ALL SEASONS

White, sprung into green.
Blue bird songs bore
the stillness.
Autumn flashed,
purple cumulus,
burned oranges, and
cinnamon aureole with
bitter edges.

Finally with her hair chopped off.
Showing her
salt scarred face.
After a long, windy dry spell.

Fecund,
west wet she was.
Til, north blue lies of snow and ice
formed white teeth.
Leaving
punctures
into the plush, pulsing red
Cardinals
cycle round
waiting,
writing,
in the long
dark bruise
between times.
Eternity
in spaces
Just before ex-and-
inhale
Waiting,
waiting,
waiting,
for the warm
golden.

THE LADY OF THE LAKE – No. 1

The lady of the lake lives
in deep blue water
Her hand reaches out
clutching the Excaliber
She waits for her knight
With the knowledge of sea
She is the lady of the night
howling out in fright, against crashing love
She is the weed that slips up to the sky,
always reaching, always seeking perfection

Bottom coral reef fish are
a cacophony of emotions that
color times when love Tsunamis near
When the sea is raging
the sand, holds hearts smashing past time
She takes courage
reaches out through the surface
While visible in this world
dwelling in the other

Great is the water
blue, green,
fire black storms raging
salty tears torn
Belly stretched
ripped hands impaled, she cries for us

She accepts the rain, it fills her
We all see the hand reaching out
filled with Excaliber
But who among us has the courage
to take the task,
slay the dragon,
stay the journey,
of blue eyed knights

She...
Lady of the lake

THE LADY OF THE LAKE — No. 2

The lady of the lake
splashing down streams
of knowledge over you.

Her surface dances
a waterfall of stars and suns
set in a deep blue
heart pool of emotions

Vibrations
forming a small ripple around her wrist
that radiates out across all waters,
concentric, around it scours the shore of time

The ripples kiss
the sanded lips
As sure as she was,
when she kissed yours.
Arthur

You were life's power
She collected shells for you
and decorated your crown
She turned your bed down
Passed through the void – pregnant
Gave bloody birth to your dreams

She came through your surface
Holding her breath
You did not have the courage
to enter her world
Deep
you split it opened
rising to the frothing surface
She is exposed,
alone
There is no Arthur
on this journey.

THE LADY OF THE LAKE — No. 3

She knows, how women wash in the morning
how their hair falls into the sink,
how they think.
Swirling whirlpool subtlety
rippled her once still surface
hiding the raging red thoughts

She carries the sword along with its radius scars
marking the equator where
they ripped apart her belly
Stretch marks where she expanded
with Arthur's dream

Her right leg
dented at the shin
is the Tigress
her left rivered
with blue tributaries
the Euphrates

At the delta is the fire of life
cradle of creation
cratered by a snipped perineum
the birthplace of all

The Ganga goddess
deliverer
destroyer
epiphany
grace
Lashing over the earth
deep blue green sea
reflecting a
tsunami of souls
On the shores of the living
She is the spirit of creator blazing
liquid bronze
poured in the sphere of time.

IF WE WERE IN LOVE – No. 1

If we were a song, we'd be sung by Aretha Franklin
If we were a poem, we'd be written by Langston Hughes,
spoken by Paul Robeson.
If we were a clear thought, we'd be an affirmation
by Thich Nhat Hanh.
If we were a river we'd be the Amazon
or the Ganges—
If we could run that way,
we'd be a Gazelle.
If we were making love
while listening to Aretha we'd be Eagles
coming together hundreds of feet in the air
Falling down
feathers entwined
falling down
breaking our embrace
only, and
at last
at impact.

IF WE WERE IN LOVE — No. 2

If there were such a thing
we would have it
Not like an object of consumption
Or for the art of decoration
No, not for positions of social power
or to satisfy some
unfulfilled narcissistic need
Not to meet some
religious right of passage ritual
or to punish each other
for our parents' pain
Nor to stave off fear
of loneliness,
or death.
No,

I can tell you
If there were such a thing
we would become
one
burning
like a blue Buddha flame
If there were such a thing
we would fly hundreds of feet up
into life
and crash together
free falling
fornicating like eagles
locked in passion's embrace
free falling

If there were such a thing
when we crashed to the earth
it would transform
a liquid purple night sky
ripples emanating from us
would radiate
throughout the dark
throwing off vibrating stars
spiraling into galaxies

If
there
were
such a thing
we would have it
pouring out of our eyes
like hot red silk over all
Filling the universe
with lovers
draped around each other
free
falling

If there were such a thing
we would have it...
It would come back to Earth
through our children
Fill the sky with blazing sun

If such
a thing
were ours
unlike the eagles
who release love's grip
just before death's impact
we would have the faith
not to let go
until we hit the earth
together
forever

STIGMATA

Yeah,
you think;
love,
it's like driving down the highway at sixty
one hand on the wheel.
In your right hand is a heart-shaped pincushion
pierced through with hat pins you've collected
in your traveling years.
You toss it up in the air just short of the roof liner.
It begins to descend toward your hand
seemingly
to you
straight up and
down.

But, to an x-wife
who was an ex-grade school English teacher
turned ex-bartender
and eventually ex-Erotic dancer
standing on the side of the highway
with a cardboard sign reading:
Anywhere but here!
For her, the bloody red
heart shaped form
rises in a slow arc moving past.
Covering nearly one hundred feet
before it begins its descent
at sixty miles an hour
stabbed through
with pins
she doesn't recognize as yours.
Gone from her sight
before it falls into your hand again.

She imagines it
impaled in you
blood trickling out from the punctures.
Leaving
a permanent mark there
in the palm of your right hand.

She thinks
yeah,
that's love for you.
Even with the stigmata
you need imagination
and faith
to get
hold of it.

RAVENS OF MOSCOW

Could I
see her eyes
sparkled hoar frost blue-grey
with centers marked of dark birds?
Could they be seen through a tangle of arms
like a forest of white birch trees
staring from her short lived face?

They peered
tied to eternity
wide
lighted by the pale silver Moscow sky
mourning
light draw

Raven shadows passed through us
Screeched, flying into our
lost place
Amid the cackle and caw

The ravens of Moscow
black and gray pallbearers
keep their silence
still, I strained my ears
to hear the muffled mystery drum
In my thoughts
I pulled against her
warm familar smell

We never touched

Even as the days of my life
passed with increasing speed
it seemed long
the shift from night to day
I watched it happen
the flowers limply piled

I felt the shadow of
the raven fall
In the daylight
I could almost taste her, hold her
pull her inside
I strained —
shook from the longing
to see the fire in her loins
sliding over her to
penetrate her depth
screaming into the whirlwind
burning
blood red
rain
the interior color
of old black Russian lacquer boxes

We never touched.

THE STARS WERE HERS

When she, like Night, was a baby
waiting for the warmth of Sun.
Unaware the stars were hers.
longing only for a glimpse of Sun.
She moaned and rushed around eyes wide.
Creating swirling trails
of star fire from her tears.

Like Night, she grew to hate her
mother Moon.
Seeing her as a mere reflection of him.
She like night, felt deceived by the telling
that Sun was her father.
He never gave his love.
He never touched.
He was never there.
Mother Moon waited, for Night's love to return.
Although Moon's feet were freezing
she suckled her child's needs before her own.

Like Night, she was a child
chilled blind with anger!
Cold, even when jagged rips of
blazing light shot through her.
Sun — Sun...
Her only audible thought
Left her dark scarred, and longing.

She aged tenfold with each solstice.
Often burning in balled blue lightning
whipped white hot by an opium delirium.
High,
she fell into a darker despair.
Dour in the cold of solar eclipsed emptiness.
She like Night often took up with strangers.
Waking up to the taste of her own blood in her mouth.

Death's smell
rising
from deep gashes
she carved in the crook of her inner arms.
Fucking dazed.
Never knowing the stars were hers.
Day, her half-brother
often tormented her
by lingering
still warm from the sun's glow.
He bragged of his power to burn.
His confidence borrowed from the Sun,
as he ran from her grasp.
Are you my father? she asked.

He laughed.
Taunting her with an erection
and empty promises of love.
Her enormous desires are bared teeth
and crimson flecked eyes
are never able to unmask
his disguised taunts
of familial love.

She like Night, was now a woman.
Who had cut her flesh and ached
to be a Nubian princess.
Parted her violated red Cleopatra lips
unable to speak.
Ripped at her heart's soft places
with razor needs.

She, like Night began to glow golden.
Out from the sliced spaces.
Forming constellations.
And more, yes more, she could dream purple.
Not a delusionary opium blur,
but with clarity and depth of vision.

An epiphany,
she could dream awake.
The crystal spark of her life
reflected in the wrinkled face
and flattened breasts of her mother, Moon.
Whom sadly she had hated.
Now joyfully cradled with love and respect.
A torrential notion of how like Moon she was
slagged in her depths.
Only Moon could set the waters in motion.

In silence she glistened.
Encompassing endless connections
of constellations.
Even now without the stranger's embrace,
she like Night, was filled with power.
With love.
The love of the warrior.
She wore it edged in fine blue sadness.
A child no more.
Like Night
she knew at last
all the stars
were hers.

GRAPES – No. 1

Truth, dare,
consequences, private
or repeat?
Shotsie chooses dare.
You must French kiss Lina DiEscola
for five minutes, no breaks.

Sliding up, I waited for her to position.
Grass staining our clothes.
Remembering, Frankie said
she had grapes in her bra.
I leaned in,
the small brown stain on her
upper lip suddenly
looked like a map of New Jersey.
Slowly, with Burt Lancaster on my mind, and
before my lips found hers
in painful slow motion
her mouth transformed
into the Grand Canyon.
My lips, teeth and tongue
fell in up to my nose.

Although I was no French expert
it all seemed far too dental to me.

My tongue darted out
like a small vole trying to escape
a menacing cat constructed
of the other kids in the circle.
Back and forth it scurried
seeking her Dr. Livingston of a tongue
in the darkest Africa
of her wet mouth.

I couldn't find it anywhere.
Finally with my under tongue cleft
ripped open.
I pulled out.
Too dumb to keep quiet
I asked to see hers
Just to be sure it existed.

There it was
sticking out of her mouth
like Lou Costello
without fedora,
and as red from Red Hot Candy
as my face.

Innocence

GRAPES — No. 2

"I love those plump red Italian Grapes."
She said.
Ovale,
I thought as I dropped
one between our lips
while we kissed.
I pulled it into my mouth
then slipped it
into hers.
She rolled it around
never scarring
its delicate skin.
I lowered myself down
mouth open
below her bottom lip
She dropped it down to me.

I pushed it along
her cheek to neck.
Down
to that spot where neck
and chest conjoin.
Rested it there
in the hollow.
"Ovale,"
I said.

Rolled it
over her hills of Tuscany breasts.
Back up her vesuvial chin
into her mouth.
There I left it.
Clenched between her teeth.
Retracing my path
down
as though
still chasing it.
Down —
whispering
"Ovale."
Down
until she bit it through.
Spraying me
with pear-shaped
slippery
seeds.

Temptation

GARDEN'S GODDESS

She is brown,
our garden's goddess
in diamond gown.
Her luscious full breasts
soaring under
summer's languid whisper
Pressing, her sweltering musk
rising up—
while I turn her over

Suckling
sweet juices
of pomegranates
explode into her mouth
Small, fire seeds
sown in the day's end
slide into mine

All gyrations
of the soils turning
between the pitchfork's tines,
spark against the raging red sun-bathed sky
Portend seasons change.
held plaintive,
in anguished clouds

Even as the fall's purple chills.
She dances, before me
in the soul's turning.
Her gown's jewels sparkled against the tines
are squeezed out of a single drop
of sweat.

I MISSED SOMETHING

No. 1

Maybe I missed something
in that glance, its icy edge
The tip of some glacier forming under our talk
"Are you OK?" I moaned, trying to establish a base camp in this climb.
We flew back up to the
"how's the weather" surface again
and smiled at each other out from a crevice
of our own making.

"Just thought I'd toss you a rope," I blurted out with this thought.
She said, with the ice pick
fracturing a lot of history between us
and of course, in a loving way.
"Fuck you!"

No. 2

    "Hey I heard you were on strike. It looks to be a long one."
I don't want to offend you, but we've known each other for thirty
years or I wouldn't ask. Although I realize I have on many occasions
tried to rekindle our friendship and you have not come round.
    Watching the news I thought of you and the new baby and the
house mortgage and decided I would extend once more and offer you
some part-time work at my place. Maybe you never forgave me for
telling you when we were 20 that your live-in girl was trying to fuck
her way through all your friends and had a habit of collecting bazookie
players from Arab bars. That kept you from responding.
Or maybe I just missed something.
    The strike ended before you could come by and make some cash
to hold you over.
    I still waited for your call.

TIME CAFÉ

Her mouth opened,
I looked inside to the soft, warm places of it.
She offered me some insight to a woman's point of view.
"It has to be her idea," she said "Men are always
trying to make things happen."
Too much yang; I thought myself clever.
We sat outside; as men sit, outsiders to a woman's power.
A table at the Time Café
We use the insane show of New York City passing us by
to measure it.
We are of different cultures, nationally, and in ways
that men and women are.
Though in us there's a glow of one world culture
of traveled depth,
Of places as indescribable as God, we talk as
our souls bounce around the outer universe at such speeds
burning up upon entering the inner.

Time

It passes under our talk, a warm, slow fertile, river

Rivers swirl my mind on silk sheets.

Drowning, I slipped under without resistance.

Thoughts of long kisses and a passionate caress.

I tried to control it. Not to show it

My mouth opened; I didn't let it out.

Even as every word that passed between us flew out and burst

exploding stars, wind swirled, lightning

lit up and thrust in the dark spaces between us.

"Just give into it," she interrupted,

"Men are always trying to control life."

I could see how other women find her irresistible.

I could see the passion in the corners of her mouth

in the dark centers of her eyes.

Her licking like a flame that could burn down the boundaries.

Sucking closed both space and time.

All the future, and past blurry with the heat —

intense enough to melt the

barriers between a man and a woman.

I wondered like all men.

How?

How does she gives herself unconditionally?

On the flat surface

of a table

at the Time Café.

THE WAY THINGS ARE

"I bought this book!" he said.
"you will like it, it's a spiritual book."
He said,
"It's five inches long and about seven inches wide
and at least three quarters of an inch wide —
deep, I mean."

I took in his darting eyes.
His arm muscles visibly twitching
under skin
covered by a tattooed dragon
of many colors.

"Yeah!" he acknowledged my glance,
"I get these tremors
from the lithium—
I take this other medicine
to stop them."
Our eyes met again
he sighed
and looked away.
I want to smash the prison
of the drugs,
To spin him deep into the source
To flash him with the fury of white
light of all the universe
reach out to warm him.
But the Dragon rose up
spiraled around the words we spoke.
consumed our lives, as it danced
between us in the silence.

I pray he opens up the book.

ABSOLUTION FOR THE
TEXAS TUMBLER

He recognized me.
The way you'd spot an old war buddy.
Across a slab of time
across the country
to across the colossal
foyer of the Hilton Hotel in Houston.

"I saw you on the tube!
I came down here figuring to see you,"
He said.
I felt him before I knew he was there.
Eyeing me from 100 feet away.
He had it.

A sign hovering huge over him
written in bright unresolved emotions
it read:

I LIVED IT TOO!

I saw the sign first this time
Long before I saw his eyes
aching for someone to help close the bloody rip
in his family circle.
Long before his warm hand slipped into mine.
"Do you know who I am ?" He said.

"Sure Jack, I know you. How could I forget,
you and your brother tumbling and flipping
around in white tights showing off acrobatic skills."
"Yeah! I guess we did show off some.
It's so great to see someone from the projects!"
he spurted. Looking past me
to see if there was any response
to that admission.
Then
he fired the next volley.

"Good old Paterson.
Remember those days!"
Underneath the exuberant words
swirled the scaled amphibians of our dark past
slithering into place.
Slipping through the reeds of time and defenses.
Gyrating in an emotional dead pile dance
to the beat of father's fists
forming a distant hypnotic pounding sound.

Perhaps Jack's acrobatic skills
were far greater than was demonstrated.
Could they have kept him on the high wire
all this time?

Maybe
he didn't have a fall that broke him.
Could it be,
that he wasn't a needy
humpty dumpty
latch onto ya kinda sap?

Then again maybe, he never stopped tumbling.
Never stilled
long enough
to hear wolves of
unfulfilled needs howl.
Moonlit phantoms
bearing feral teeth
of lost loves, failed pursuits
bruised and bloodied drunken knuckles,
drug induced vacancies or
betrayal by false friends
and gods!

"How

could

I forget

Jack."

Later Jack's reptile trinity
of anger, guilt, and fear showed up
Relentlessly pissing them out after
too many beers.
Telling anyone nearby
between flips and tumblers
who would listen,
but only war buddies really knew.
The story had his heart pounding
again.
The words squirting out of him
something like projectile vomit.
Recounting the smell of fear and the
metal taste in his mouth.
As his
drunken
raging father
struck his mother
with his
failed husband,
absent father,
poor provider fists!

Jack's mother and he
were stunned
by the blows
and again stunned
until,
to Jack's surprise it was
his father
who tumbled to the floor
in front of him.
Purple twisted gin-soaked face
pressed to the green linoleum.
Grasping his chest
kicking his feet against
the washing machine
leaving
black heel scrapes
on its white face.

Leaving black
heel
scrapes.

Jack was slipped into his room
door closed.
Right outside
his father lay dead.
He had his hand on the door knob
many times in that
endless
few hours.
Just a boy!

You were just a boy Jack!

You could not have your father
in life
or death!

Flipping
through a box of tissues
with tears tumbling down
his 45 year-old face and
conjuring up a half smile.
Grasping a tumbler of gin
Jack rolled out to me.

"Ya know it's funny, in all this time.

All I could think about

were

the black

marks

he made."

THROWING STONES

Hey, Cookie!
Hey, Cookie!
the words jumped out of my mouth
to the rhythm of my sped up heart.
That sound
Cookie
had watermelon juice
running down my neck.
While I spit out the seeds of his name
my tongue swelled with memories.

Full with times
when the smell of sticky,
running melon sugar
stained a ripped tee-shirt
and was red, safe, and warm.

His face grimaced
but it wasn't the black, too skinny,
too tight, neck-tie knot, lost
in a yellow '60s high-roll collared shirt.
Nor the muddy green six button iridescent jacket.

"My name is Car'men," he growled.
What? Not even Kar-Mine, like his
squat, balding, hard-ass
father had called him when he was pissed off.
He was always pissed off.

I remember his father's head:
it topped off a tree-trunk body,
moved on down an indiscernible neck
bespeckled with dark, thick-rimmed glasses,
with moles of various weights,
heights, and colors.
I twinged a little nervously
seeing the old pain form on his face.

That
name
Cookie
It was Cookie DeSimone
I wanted to see.
"Ahh, hmm. Yes. Well, Carmen,
you'll always be Cookie to me—
come on, Carmen, lighten up
What are you up to now?"
Slipped from my mouth
as my hand reached out tentatively

Radiating red carmethine, he told me
that he was the floor manager
in the paint department at Rickles,
While I, surrounded by
cans of paint, and rainbows of memories
arcing back to all those glory days
in the Brook Sloate projects
When Cookie DeSimone
hit a baseball.

Not only did it go over the fence,
it seemed to rise above the plateau
that bordered the field—
rising,
rising out of our sight,
rising still.

"Well that one's a goner!" PD would chatter.
"Datsta way, boss!" he'd whine
He always called Cookie "Da Boss."
We understood.
Cookie's searing pain erupted
far more often,
far more violently than ours.
We were all scared shitless of Cookie.

We all knew it was his rage,
his love-hatred of his father,
embarrassment at living in the projects.

Not good enough!
not good enough for his dad,
not capable of feeling
the joy of his age
that drove that ripped white ball
over the hill.

All that,
collected in his pockets like so many
jagged edged throwing stones.
Together with Mary Janes, their paper wrappers
welded tight, bent bottle caps,
and dog-eared Maris–Mantle cards.

Nobody hit 'em like Cookie,
not even Joe Boy or Andy Salmon.
Any ball and a bat,
pinky and a broom stick,
branch and an uncollected rock.
Cookie DeSimone was gonna make it!
PD toll us so.

We wanted him to:
Be a baseball star!
We all glowed, mulberries in the sun
so ripe with hope for him.
We wanted him to:
Empty his pockets,
Rise, over his hatred,
rise out of our sights
over the plateau of pain
that bordered our lives
Rising still.

Cookie DeSimone,
Cookie DeSimone
now a manager
in the paint department at Rickles
Still weighted down at forty-five
with his pockets full of shame.

PATERSON 1958

I loved that car
except when he had the wheel.
Down the block, out of the Brook Sloate projects
Past the abandoned barracks into the sandlot
that became Buckley Park.
I'd see it watching me.
Although it was my
pristine stalker
like him.
I loved that car;
the smell of the place.

Lying below the back window
in the Totowa drive-in,
looking all during the film
for a falling star.

Sure, he showed it to me
in 3-3 Christina Place,
Paterson
No ancient rituals of manhood passed between us.
No family pride or honor related.
Only a driven wedge.
A homely, boney, raw wooden door stop
Not to hold open the door for
the honeysuckled air, emotions,
or friends, but to keep it shut tight.
His gift, my legacy came.
Drawing it to my chest
I must have mistaken it for the sun
it being a bright yellow, silent companion.
Only now I know it by name
Fear.
Still, at times
it is a close friend.
This, when all I really wanted was
that car of his.

He could hear me,
see me, everywhere, always
like the concave eyes on the plaster head
of Jesus, that sat on my grandmother's dresser;
"Stop trying to be someone!"
the motor roared.
The grill grimaced at me.
"Get in the car!" he'd say.
Red flames of shame
shot out of the pink and white '58

Well, why not you say.
After all he lived in it.
It was his Irish Catholic
hammer and screwdriver.
His knife and fork,
His canned creamed corn on white bread,
His pencil and pen, his gun, club, badge
blue shirt, and pants.
His scarred flesh, black spit-shined
shoes and heart.

Relentlessly reminded,
his car, his house, his bastard child secret.
Bouncing from low paying job to fired
Like a knobby turtle back cuss.
I only saw his head pop out
a smile, it seems, maybe once.
Only for others, never for us.
His joy it seemed was to sneak up on foot or
in that pink and white '58 Chevy Belair.
and catch me.
Always when I was swinging the club of fear
intimidating, some other.
Never realizing, till later,
The suffering of my mother.
The suffering of my mother.

He is still rolling that Chevy
around a shadow
past my dreams.
His skill
nurtured the fear
like a farmer
fed, stroked, and planted deep
watering with tears
sparked it
A pyromaniac, until
it was given
hot self esteem.
It stuck in my throat
when I wanted to sing.
When I ached for revenge.
It purred low,
then screamed
deafening for years
any chance of hearing
love from others.
Buzzing high-toned,
like the ringing in the ear cuffed
Droning out
corrupt moral lessons

My heart numbed slowly
while the words were sung, mantra
like a new age spiritual type without
any real faith in their power
were chanted:
You can't hurt me.
You can't hurt me.
I won't let you.
I was ashamed
for feeling
alone.

EVEN SO

Even though,
I was doin sixty on a six lane
Like usual.
That is — even when I'm not drivin.
Meaning by the way,
when life has the wheel.
Not to say that,
that keeps it even.

And, although, my tennis eyes
volley back and forth
try to slow down the scene while
straining for clues to my past.
Even in the blur of constricting pupils
over the uneven rooftops of
my Paterson.
There is clarity conjured
even without my glasses.
The parallel shingled
Germanic brick factories
now painted bright blue
and the majestic city hall dome
dummed down with paint
and layers of corruption, could
even afford
me a break.

Meaning by the way
a respite
a rest stop between life's
even and odd numbered
mile markers.

I sensed they,
meaning the secrets
were there in my cosmic womb
my birth home Paterson.
Whose visage offered itself up
for me.
A needy speeders
overview
at sixty on a six lane.
My head, hand,
turned out
through the open window.

Even though tired.
windblown, and bleary eyed
I kept it going, yes —
kept it in the lane
only occasionally
nicking the white road dashes
zippin by like friendships,
or even love.

Paterson whirred by
despite my
need to slow her down,
to peel off her mysterious clothes
of time
suckle her breasts for my pleasure.
Even so, it eluded
just out of reach
like most desires.

I wanted,
I wanted to bare her old
red
brick
heart
with its many cracks and breaks.

Her refusal to give over to me
to seduce my spirit with
stories of passion
that could set my soul
on a corrected course,
and all the collected damage
to us both, reflected on her
scarred legs closed tight.
Could not diminish
the burning need
we both carry.
Even doin sixty on a six lane
Like usual
that flashed
me passed her like after sex
conversation on deaf ears.
Even
so.

EVERLAST

Mr. Andrews pulled on the dark red
ten ounce Everlasts.
set against a slash of white
in a blue world.
Overlooking
the Brook Sloate Projects
in Paterson,
New Jersey.

He spoke sportsmanship
Prayers, we figured
for the corrupt fathers
who spoke them into the July 1965 swelter.

The fight about to begin
I considered: We're on the same baseball team
even though the black players
huddle together on the far end of the dugout.
We were mates
Yet under their boxed brim hats
lurked a stalking.
knowledge that even at the bottom
white rung
I could access places
they only watched sliding by on the disturbed surface
of the murky blood brown Passaic river
passing the ball field.

Their young baseball lives
spiked with loud sounds
Like "Go getem Satchel."
Painfully plied, nearly
out of ear shot sounds
like "Coon"
I stared into Barry's eyes
my hands sweating,
burning for the first blow to be thrown.

I remembered
Someone at the ball game
callin Barry, Satchel Page
Barry's head leaned forward
to the crowd
whose
bared arms
danced over a
hot chain link fence.
Vicious, euphemisms slithered
out of their mouths
like dorsal fins through
the dark undercurrent
in a red
sea of separation.

Mouthing inaudible curses,
through tight teeth
at thirteen.
Barry spat, what looked to me,
like blood
lost in the red dirt.

Mr. Andrews blew a spit-spattering whistle
leaving small dark blue stains in the dust.
As I slid my best Paterson shuffle up
diddy bopped around
half draggin my right foot behind
hands held low and cool
as Barry's.

Toe to toe.
"Yeah! I know how to Shotgun, I shouted,
Jr. Wells and the All-stars was on my
Victrola too!"
We weave a Barry Gordie silent slow dance round.
Shattered by:
"Get your Goddammed hands up
this ain't no block party dance!"

"Yes Mr. A n d r e w s,"
we sang in two part harmony.
Motown choreographed by a
A jab,
tentative
a jab.

"Kill the honky!" taunted Barry's older brothers
while boxing blue shadows.
Barry's left arm shot out —
Smokin with — I ain't no thief mother fucker!
streaming off of it!
Stabbing out a red Everlast
bigger than his head.

Man, I can wiggle wobble
dance a ching a ling
so I slipped under that jab
and all its rage.

Unlike Barry who couldn't
dodge his father's drunken slaps,
nor duck Antonio the grocer who was always
following him around the deli
next to School Five callin' him a thief.

"God-dammed uncolo — melanzana!"
"petty thief — eggplant!"

Barry's twisted face — screaming —
"Fuck you — you — Fat dago pimp!

While I slipped under and
snatched all I could
off the Hostess shelf
and bolted out
white,
unsuspected.

I ducked again
Under Barry's left arm
exploding with the legacy of his angry father
who at thirteen saw
his grandfather
William Fulbright Jackson
hanging
K
K
K
limp from a tree.
leaving a spit-spattered
dark spot on the sun
of a sweltering
July day in
Alabama.

Barry's jab snubbed against my shoulder.
I hooked my left hand,
burning up in that Everlast,
to his mid-section.
With the knowledge of
my rock hard —
Irish famine surviving —
great grandfather —
James Nina Gorman
Who beat Jack Levy barefisted
in New Orleans in 1865.

Before he could
recover, I stunned him
with a combination rising up —
catching chin —
clamping
his
teeth
tighter still.
like a
slip knotted
hemp
rope of memories.

My right hand now lay in wait
in the purple shadows.
Like my Neopolitan grandfather
Joseph Casperino
Smelling of Dinobli stogies and grappa did
for the loan shark,
come to collect
my uncle Butch's unpaid debt.

Grandpa
a giant with white slicked down hair
had paws like Antonino Rocca.
He hit that shark in the head
with Rocca's hands
I thought...
they couldn't be his hands.
The ones;
that caressed my face softly,
and held me high and firm
to see the bocci players argue.
The ones;
that so deftly pinched the edges of ravioli,
and picked the fine silk threads
passing them to the George Street silk mill bobbins

Joseph
unleashed his right
then left —
First the shark's legs
then his
life!
Fell from him
like the brown flush of a toilet
onto the South Paterson sidewalk
in front of me.

Grandpa
left me there
ran down the block,
ran,
ran,
ran to Naples.

Returning to Paterson
years later
as Francis Nicholoro
Second hand family in tow.
How my mother cried.

Small spirals of dirt memories
rose at our feet,
set against a slash of white
in a blue world.
As my right hand
launched from its lair
Barry was filling up with
a brutish
purple festering
puss filled rage!
He swore to kill me!

Barry's right hand
panther sprung
in a swift arc
Coming with
Nat Turner's faith
in the righteousness of its bloody purpose.
Exactly at the same instant
we made contact with each others faces.

Both our heads thrown back
by the sheer force
of our wills.
Streams of the same rich
ancestral crimson
poured out of our noses in a
salty clear mix
fell to the dust.
Both of us stunned
back into ourselves.

Barry and I became aware
of the laughter around us.
Mr. Andrews stepped in
hands on our shoulders
grinning a huge grin asking us to shake hands,
commending us on a good fight,
echoed by the hooting crowd.

We looked far too tired
and battered
for thirteen
Smiling at each
we came together over the divide
of being other.
Embraced, at last as bloodied teammates
in the game of life.
The only thing between us
from then on,
was a friendship which would,

everlast,   everlast,   everlast...

Gorman, Andrews Homer,
PBA Defeats B.S., 3-0

A Hug For His Homer

POOL HALL

I played pool with the dead!
Same as always
My rough skin clung to me in the thick smoke
like blood-soaked wool —
Stinking, sour mildew of recognition
came in three gun shots
while surrounded by cigar spit and body sweat odor
swirling, the dimly lit room roared
A loud, crack! crack! crack!

Filled with slate slabs
under stretched green cloth
with holes in it,
Same as the holes in my shirt,
Same color as the cloth they covered
me with in the OR, I thought,
as my balls were being pulled through it,
Two of 'em painted like the five,
bright, orange orange orange

Red mahogany rails pocked dark
by burning cigarettes
The players set on stained benches
with hard faces, lighted by the glow
of a granny ash dangling,
Playing out a darker dark
As they hack! hack! hack!

The sun and moon are a cue ball
In this skyless world of
grit and grime made grimly blue
by a chalk dust swirl sent up
with the felling of a crumpled life
A buck for the man boy Tony
who racks! racks! racks!

Carlos has got the moves down,
weaseling his way into a lock
He's tango tongued and alligator supple
 Gotta figure Tony boy wantsta drop
 that buck in his pocket
 Tony boy gets offered the five—
 "Carlos gonna give me the fa-fa-five?"
 He stuttered, stuttered, stuttered.

I played pool with the dead
Same as always
Sprawled my life
the color of the seven,
fast spreading out on the wooden floor
I try to hold it with a little draw,
but all I can feel are the
Cracks... cracks... cracks...

Shocking

PROZAC MEMORIES

Prozac memories
Kodak emulsion
fade
I saw
they had small scalloped edges
folded at the corners
of your mouth
Spilling out images
Those telling stories of
youthful excesses
Cut short
Tucked under
Black corners
with glue
trying to
hold them
tight
in your
album

POLAROID

Beauty's
picture
and
love
recall

an elaborate
need beneath,
an enormous emptiness

Melancholy

OCCUPIED LANDS

Sprawled lifeless Bonnie and Clydes
Raccoons
with their teeth showing,
small arms reaching up
are stiffened, eviscerated barricades in
the life versus high-tech machine
passion play

Played out on a gauntlet
black expanse of road.
Brightly dappled with
yellow autumn light.
Wearing a victory wreath of
red leaves stained,
by a murder of crows.
and small creatures,
lottery running.

All live in occupied lands
the Palestinians of the American highway
Their myths
destroyed
their culture and language
negated
All sympathizers labeled
eco-terrorists
by zealots of the auto cult
wanting more power,
land,
and shining metal
security
Their furred poets
no longer Emerson-ecstatic
can only rhyme of war.

A war of attrition
Darkly
time rings around the eyes
of coons
Squirrels have anxiety attacks
Eating nuts until
they vomit uncontrollably

Beaver warnings have become
indecipherable signals
They no longer slap down on the
front porch in the morning
bringing white news of refreshing water places

Text on the daily pages like
cynical swarms of black crows,
swash and
bite out the few Blue Bird
skies
with false tales.
Truth,
crushed under the weight
of profit
Rabbits!...
We all live in occupied lands

Righteousness

ON THE RUN

Blasting along Route 17
One of the many
The cumulus bottoms burst into flames

Poets are thieves
on the run.
I considered.
Stealing lines
from someone
else's
face.

NAMING

I considered that religion
was an illness of naming.
Like the science it denied.

Its naming labeled each
Stamen and pistil
Labia and Glans
Each wind and rain
Passion and poem

A wealthy patron's paid
cartographer of shame,
that never leaves the drawing board.
Who traces his blind abilities with joy at
marking each of us like Cain.
While never
naming
love.

MISTRESS OF JUDGMENT

Heat shimmied up my pants leg
as I walked toward the court administrator
"Plan for a long day," she advised
exhaling smoke from her dark,
passion-pursed Latin lips.
She enticed, in blazing-yellow, too-tight clothes
that clung to her in a Tango grip.
My eyes followed up slowly,
from the black, sun flashing, spiked heel shoes —
Roughly wrinkling the yellow as I went.
Pliant black leather zippers, belt and bag.
I told myself, I should suck
the rest of her breath from her mouth.
She has power.

The smoke rose humorously,
to the sign above her that read
Health Center — just next to the brick-faced
county courthouse,
her smoke twisting up in the air
like the illusion of justice and freedom in America.
As she unfolded her arms and leaned forward
I look for the lines of her underwear.

The American dream smoke rising before me in irony.
A vision it seems only artists can acquire
Others glean theirs only from the TV,
their sexual pleasure gathered from
the disasters of others.
They have no power.

In the perverse America
The imagination is strapped tightly
by the dominatrix of a culture.
Never allowing anyone to come.
Today, in this courthouse
My eyes searched for her nipples
through the flash of color.
They
Pledge allegiance
promise to be good soldiers
Sanctimoniously follow protocol and call it justice.

I wanted her —
America that is — to wake up to herself
wanted to fuck her into a passionate frenzy,
to set her free to live the life of the imagination
I am dragged Today
True self
gagged, into the vortex of
restraints I live beyond.
I am to be judged today.
Erect,
when all of my life has been a struggle
not to.

GYPSY SHAMAN-KNOWING

Her eyes came round to me
I beckoned her to look
Feeling heat from the
blazing red sun in the black sky
Sparks flashed in the blue
void of her eyes

It was hard to tell if it was
terror
surrounding her, or the
purple shawl pulled over her head,
trimmed in a gold pattern
too delicate to see,
that held me staring

Nor am I sure
when, exactly,
I saw the other figure
that strode at her side was
much older and exotic
perhaps a gypsy shaman with
knowing

Under the purple shawl
her translucent skin
remembered the pain
of life with a tattoo
on her turning neck

For that
I looked closer
In my ghost walks,
In my small death,
Longing for the significance of life
here in my visions

The tattooed circle was in black
with a cross at its center of red and blue.
Was this the cross of Georgia O'Keefe
or Pilate's?
A medicine wheel?
More a mathematical equivalent of the earth
on its axis, a talisman
pointing her spirit
in the four directions.

How could the sky be so black?
I knew this blazing red sun
was a hole in the surface of the earth
to look up through
This blazing fire ball
a small window.
Like that of Camus' "Stranger"
Would this light resurrect?
I asked her.
What could I not know
of gypsy knowing?
Walking alone
how could it be denied me?

My sight took her in ravenously
my mouth
jealously considered
her companion,
Who whispered comforting psalms
only for her ears.
Placing a radiant balance in her walk.

Asking of her in a silent scream,
if it was terror, or the purple shawl of night
that gave her access to grace
in the face of a terrible fate?
As her face slipped from view,
and the red window closed.
I fell deeper into
the earth.
Still not knowing.

HOW DO YOU DO?

I fuckin' kill people for a living.
That's right,
Take a good look.
Look into the eyes of a killer.
I am the shaman you fear.
I kill off the old ways.
Your old suffering, the one you cling to in your
false security, kicked out.
It's never what you think it will be.

Is it?

None of the illusions you build up
about people by the cars,
hair, clothes, color of skin,
or manner of speech, work here.

Do they?

Smell the wet electric of it?
This is a place of your deepest panic.
Your secret plunging abyss
turned out bare.
"He seemed such a regular guy, He watched TV
he was white, he even wore the same watch as me."

Face it!

It's never quite skewed your way.
You know what I mean;
the kind of love you think you want.
The position you think you deserve.
The partner you created in your head
from the twisted images
your mother and father
burned you with.

The food, of which there is never enough
doesn't taste like it should.
The money never, the sex as you dreamed
never
filling in the dark razor slices in your heart.
I can mark you,
for all the world to read in awe or
fear or loathing
like a permanent tee-shirt slogan.
I can cut you,
dripping your life's blood
free from all of it.

How   do   I   do ?

I never stalk
I wait here for you,
the walking wounded.
I never have to go out and search.
You find me.
You start off flashing your Seville Row suits.
The Tiffany rings,
Gucci bags filled with the pain
and illusions,
that governments
ask young men to die for.

You are superficially drawn here
at first by a bloodthirsty,
fashion slash news propaganda
PR machine that moans out social trends
and grinds up
the hearts of the people and delivers
them to me in Mercedes.
You roll up shining.

Don't you!

Then, in an instant there is
the searing painful awareness that you are
confronting the demise of
your old self.

Reflecting in the rearview mirror
Your heart pounding, eyes searching
for the signs of my part in this death.

I look like you!

No bones in the nose.
Scars all well hidden inside.
No Harley engine torn apart in the lobby,
no beer-swilling, filthy
slob of indifference.

Oh my God!

Look into the eyes of a killer
and find yourselves.
Fretting, such fear
"Oh my God! You say.
What will I have after giving up the judgments,
The illusion of endless youth, and finally accepting
old age sickness and death."

Your Death!

Tastes like your tongue crossing nine volt battery terminals
the metal blue sparked power
filling the nostrils when the machines light up.
Current passes through our bodies
at the point where we touch.
It drags us into the
black bowels of the earth — searching
for the Badger animal
whose sharp claws and needle teeth
slash out — eviscerating you
In a healing, blood gash, rite of passage,
your old self as doomed to death — as your body!

I rip up the skin and reveal the raw emotions
binding us all together.
The sour mildew of fear screaming
Trying to tell just one person
of the battleground within.

Or perhaps in the death rattle
the taste of victory
over your struggle.

How do I do?

By slinging colors in the grooves.
I shaman massage the primal need to suffer,
close the circle of inner angst,
all at once
injure
heal
and mark.

Giving the phoenix life to the divorcée
who cut off her social, sex signal, long hair,
and told the world
she refused to allow her husband
to beat her between fuck sessions.
She is the one who finally has
control of her body.

I have my methods,
some your favorite things
at hand.
I use machine technology
to kill.
After all, you, of all people
should be comfortable with that.

I've slashed many on CNN to your enjoyment.
When I engage my machines
they vibrate spark and tap
into thousands of years
of the most base emotional
outpourings of human kind
disguised as acts of divine guidance.

This is your death!

All illusions of immortality peel away the
reminders of our impermanence spill out with the
trickle down of a dark red psyche you try to deny
by diverting our attention to the sky.
Wiping up all the evidence and confusing the crime
 scene with theological propaganda.

Look closely !

I close the circles of mourning for
dead loved ones with scalpel precision.
Lopping off the last joint
of the fifth digit on the left hand.

I never asked for your fucking opinion!

I
carve
out
feral images of sub-conscious yearning
on your hide.

With long stainless steel tapered points
I slash through the skin in tender places.
I slash through the fat layers of lies,
false pride and profits.
I whack out the Martha Stewart bullshit.
I kill off the old Republican conservative
anal retentive modernist.

Dance with me!

I release the primal beast
cut it clean in bloody ecstasy
naked and fucking
filled with love
in awe of the universe.
Finally —
and- without- pretensions- of being
separated from-
God!

DANTE'S HANDS

OR THE LONG WAY OUT
OF THE SHORT CUT

"I put my hands through hell" he said
Standing stoop shouldered, fingernails as black as his Harley tee
Ponytail long and ragged as the flat black 76 FLH,
held together by sheer luck
like his existence.
His woman cackling louder than the motor
pulled her eyes open so wide I swore her optic nerve
was on the verge of being as exposed
as the rest of her nerves were,
her bare chatter changing subject matter
without a signal light.
Speeding through
so as not to be responsible for her ideas.
She revealed the most mundane details of her relationships
the way you'd drop change in a toll booth.
Spilling out names that rang of fiction to me.
I toll her, "I really don't know who these people are
and I am not sure what you're saying."
She blurted out,
"Why, of course not, you silly ass!"

I tried to look beyond the surface.
I tried to send out calm into the room.
I waited for it to settle.
Her eyes closed, showed a flash of violet blue
just before the lids got slammed together.
Yeah, yeah she whispered, "I was born again...
yeah, Christian; then he started for Christ's sake
drinkin'and gettin' high,
so there it went."
I remember the suffering in life;
I tried to see the humanity.
Man was I glad when they left.

MARLBORO MAN

Chunks of gold comprised his monogram ring. Dazzling gold surrounded his wrist in a pile of watchband and bracelets. The yellow metal seemed almost as out of place in his mouth as on his gnarled hands, tattooed with indecipherably fuzzy blue letters. Each digit's symbol led your eye to the web of thumb and forefinger of his right hand, where the stigmata of a long forgotten commitment read to love Joan forever. If only he'd held onto Joan the way he clutches that cigarette, his life might have been different. Though not necessarily better. Those hands might have been better suited to the simple battered wedding ring of the day laborer or the scarred but unpretentious absence of decoration of a convicted felon.

It wasn't until the flash of his smile that I reconsidered. Sparkling gold teeth shone out of his mouth. They lit up his whole face, until a cloud of cynical stories and blue-gray cigarette smoke passed over it. A life of dirty deeds, boonswaggles and seductions leapt out of his deep-pocketed blue eyes. I tried to focus and breathe in the billowing smoke, the stinking rancid barbecue in the trash and bleak commentary that poured out of him. I wanted him to let out his life to me. Maybe he literally was. Continue the interview rang my mantra. "Well, Bud, after half a century of being in the skin trade if you could do it over what would you do differently? How would you have changed it?"

A riotous cough sent him doubling over, his body retching in what seemed a desperate, convulsive cry for help. I was suddenly aware of how tight and dark the waiting room was.

"Goddamn — egh! Emphysema," he gagged out. He started up again "Well you know, son, let me tell ya." Bud prefaced every gem of wisdom with this phrase. I heard it over and over. It was his way of slamming you with a two-by-four to get your attention. It made me think at the moment, of the music in Jaws. "I've been in the skin trade for as long as I can remember." He sputtered again, spasming into a long cough.

"Are you all right Bud?"

"Yeah I'm fantastic." "Ain't Life Grand," done in a 1930s Texas Swing style, twanged from the ceiling speakers — Bob Wills and the Texas Playboys, offering their ironic commentary here in Arlington, Texas, out of a dark 1990s box. Bud sat up, his right hand tapping the pack of butts in his blue short-sleeve poplin shirt. He tapped, then again, just to be sure they were there. He took the pack out, tapped it on the counter, pushed the bottom corner up, forcing out several cigarettes just enough so the configuration of filters exactly resembled those in the old Marlboro ads. Out slid a butt. He tapped it on the filter side with his tattooed right hand. He moved so deftly, sliding the pack into his shirt, it seemed one motion to me. I had seen it so many times over the last few hours that I'd become enthralled by the ballet. It was almost a Baryshnikoff move. Again he tapped the pack. He seemed to lose consciousness for the entire period of this dance. He sniffed the butt then lit it so fast I missed it. "Well, you know son, let me tell ya. If I had to do it all over again, I'd've been a preacher."

BEDS – No. 1

"You remember don't you?
You made this bed.
Yellow headboard bolted to the wall.
You picked out of the rip
white batting,
thinking of snow.
Stuffed it into
the neck of Smokey The Bear.
Keeping his head upright
to watch for—
The fires of the inevitable."

"Yeah, you remember.
The bed of rocks you kneeled on
in the dry creek of
Molly Ann's Brook, Paterson.
Turning colors daily
from the
dye house spew.
Your
spit soaked
red wool gloves
froze to the bridge's steel grey bottom rails
as tight as our mouths."

"Yess, yes.
The one in Calle — yess,
that forced the two of us tightly together
More of a hammock
its bottom expanding through the wooden rails
like your womb.
We sweat that night like a hangover
before the long train ride
to Paris drunk on each other."

"You made this bed. Now you sleep in it.
you said;
This bed of nails
one for each word
left unsaid."
You considered, that the Fakir
in Benares
could withstand the pain of its points
Breaking concrete blocks over his heart.
He heard the hammer fall.
So could you.

"You made this bed."
Dragged it bound to you
up Agung, fire navel of the earth in Bali.
Slid it down the Himalayas
forcing the two of you
into illegal border crossings.
Slipping by
stoic
Chinese
emotion guards.
Tied it behind your sagging
Chevy, by a thin thread of thought.
A minimalist expression of order
in the chaos.
Cracking your head
on the head board
rushing down
the Colorado's rapids
of ecstatic, erotic white water.
Screaming out!
"YOU MADE THIS BED!..."

BEDS – No. 2
(THE SMELLS)

Four swollen hours for 25 bucks.
The Royal Motel's beds were kept tidy,
save for the cockroaches,
by groups of lesbian maids
who always seemed to be sending up spiraling
signals of smoke.
One in mouth and other in ashtray burning.
This was years before paganism was hip.

They managed
to keep the pill-covered chenille bedspreads
from tearing.
Despite the fact you could read
the lines in a patron's face through them.
Always, they left a mixture of
pessimism, Pine Sol, and smoke in their wake.
Slow blue ripples,
coming and going.
Counting the sheets as inventory
of rooms used in a day.

That was when I,
as artist in residence
smirked.
Sitting behind the desk
taking in the cash
for rooms, while I
leered at the
circus of humanity
passing through the seedy
Art Deco portals
of this adult pleasure palace.

Could this be me? I thought.
Smelling of Canoe.

As I pulled my car around
filled with a date
to gather time in a
free room.
A bonus of counting heads
At the Royal.

Royal.
She was affectionately
called by those who knew
the sounds of her infidelities.
Royal.
She also rang an off-key clang
as home for a transient family.

He, well over six feet
staggering in at 150 pounds,
bearded and toothless
say for one stub hanging
where his left bicuspid would have sat.
His head arched back
and off-centered
above yellow stained rife armpits
where seemingly useless willow arms
attached along
to a deeply curved spine jutted out.

She, struggling to get to five feet
dusted with Hostess Cupcake crumbs
weighing in at around the volume of
the crumpled, multi-colored,
three wheeled, and one-rimmed
Volkswagen they had.
It never ran.
She never sat in it.

Two or three kids
I couldn't tell
there were always more it seemed
when the door opened slightly
and never on time to pay the rent.

The Cash was always ripped and worn
it had as many colors spotted on it
as the faces of the kids.

Royal my ass!
Surrounded in a very cool
fifties kidney-shaped light
that beamed, buzzing
Always smelling of
ozone.
She rose like a fart in church.
A boil on the ass of the community.
A flea bag — whore house!
The cops would call it
when they rode past
the plastic flowers covered in road dirt
in their black and whites red lights flashing
to an S&M scene gone bad.

But never,
never said a bad word
about her
when they pulled in
smiling, for free rooms
in their station wagons.
Flashing bands of white skin
around the third finger of left hand
at the end of bare tattooed arms
strung too tight around,
too young
girls
dressed in pink uniforms
smelling of
Remington gun oil
and Dunkin Donuts.

The neon light slithered
across Route Three
in Seacaucus New Jersey.
Former center of pig farms in the Garden State.
Now home to retired teamsters.

It was the kind of place
people from Princeton didn't even see
with darkened windows rolled up tight and locked
smelling of Gucci water
as they roamed
for the Mercedes dealerships.

This smoky canyon of beds
was the flagship property of an MD
who always smelled of vitamins,
and rubbing alcohol.
Who was always raging
red-faced about
stretching the sheets
and losing his money at the track.
He would later lose it all:
his license to practice.
Something about swapping
prescriptions
for sex, and then finally
his life.

Two shots
in the back of the head.
Coffined in the trunk of his
'78 deco green Coupe DeVille
The last of the big Caddies
with a padded white half roof
and opera lights lit.
They found him
with a halo
of bloody scripts

This Royal miasma
was managed by a cigar
and garlic breathed,
seriously short, balding ex-cop
with a taste
for bisexual women,
who had sado streaks for
black alligator belts size 48.

An Italian American captain,
busted off the force
by the shifts in the political winds
that kept payoffs
from Passaic County mobsters
to police brass
from being
acceptable.

After all
it really
was the gambling,
racist white cops
and premature ejaculating
politicos
smelling of Brute
sitting in Catholic church basements
with piles of cash at the table and
surrounded by pistols
with their identifying
serial numbers
sanded off
"Throw away's"
like their souls,
and their junk-riddled informants
who made this Royal world of dark purple
smoke go round.

I can still smell
the gunpowder
and hear
the two shots echo out
in the courtyard of the Royal.
Every time I am wrapped in a ripped
chenille bedspread
soaked in the sweat
of blue steel
faded mornings.
Surrounded in the
smell of
Pine Sol
and pessimism.

THE MIRACLE BIRTH OF LOU COSTELLO

Bernardo Bertolucci sat in a black metal folding chair.
Sunlight streamed in from all around. Swarming nearby is a faint odor
of coffee. He is a smile beaming out of the back of an open sunlight
silver panel truck. Though he is not alone he appears to be. Even
though there is an infinite shadow sitting near his other self.

I too am sitting, sun warmed, at his feet trying to survey his view.
I wondered at his loneliness. He, like many artists is not speaking
the vague language of the muddled middle. He is not frightened by
the ambiguity, nor does he blur the meaning of the profound.
Perhaps this sets him apart, keeps him alone.

His eyes and my own slip down mist-swept dark green hills;
I followed his eyes rolling to a view of the three cities that lay below.
One modern and the others from antiquity, all in ruins in the
fertile valley. Behind the crumpled site and breathlessly red,
rose Garret Mountain, Paterson.
For the first time it appeared to me as a mountain.

I didn't feel the need to speak cynically of Garret Hobart or denounce
the British patriarchal Lamberts. Suddenly it seemed unnecessary to
tell of the Wobblies meeting in the Botto House for the great 1914
labor strike although, this would have made him smile. Nor did I
need to tell of Ginsburg, William Carlos Williams, Demuth, and of
course the birthplace of Lou Costello. Not even that could boost the
splendor of the purple Passaic Falls and Garret in red flannel, rising.

Vaguely aware of movement, I see men, hundreds of them moving
around in the apocalyptic cityscapes. They are clad in ambiguous
dress. At once ragged American Military and Ancient Japanese
Samurai gear.

Ah! an Akira Kurosawa, homage I thought. This supposed insight on my
part like the miracle birth of Lou Costello, I never mentioned to
Bernardo. By now I had become so fascinated with the power of the
red mountain I lost my conscious contact with him. Finally Bernardo
broke the silence and spoke directly to me.

"Can one normally see the mountain in Paterson so clearly?"
I twinge at the thought of Garret juxtaposed to the Alps, I mumbled
insecurely. "No it's usually much smaller." Although I was thrilled he
should ask me anything. That same feeling of being small and from
Paterson crept in. I found myself asking a question.
"What interests a great film master like you in the sad face of Paterson.
It is really not like, say Tuscany. Really, it's not much of a landscape."

"Landscape!" He bellowed as he rose up to his feet. His arms raised
with hands palms pointed south toward the mountain. His arms
moved slowly apart till the palms faced East and West. From a black
cross of Bertolucci emanated the word. "Landscape,— No, no, no, this
is no landscape my friend. It is a metaphor," As he proclaimed his
hands moved in a Roman Tai Chi, "Capito? A metaphor for a
woman's inner emotional life. A landscape — no, this is far more
complex than a man."

I looked intent on seeing the metaphor. Closing my eyes halfway to
see it flatten. Staring through a grid opening my eyes wide, taking off
the top of my head, turning loose my creative senses, pulling down
my pants and sticking out my tongue for a clue.

Don't look directly at it I thought. Look through it. It will come clear.

In the warm sun I could smell coffee, not myrrh while in the compa-
ny of this mystery. I was startled out of bliss by the twisted dirty face
of one of the film extras leaning over a wooden horse. A ripped net
dangling off of the GI helmet that capped his scarred and muddied
face. His chins squashed tight between samurai slatted wood chest
protectors and bulbous nose. The net swings back and forth over his
small, close-set eyes as his head wags, panting. I tried to look into his
eyes that darted away at each attempt. His plump face was weighted
with the suffering of fitful sleep. Attached at the waist and rising
behind him there is a long thin black pole reaching up twenty feet,
topped off by a salmon colored flag with a black-crested imprint of a
fish and a loaf of bread. His speech twanged:

"Scuse me Mr. Bertolucci" Taking off his helmet in deference exposed
a crown of woven crabtree thorns that were cutting into his flesh,
forcing out small drops of blood that trailed mud and make-up
behind them. Dribbling down past his eyes.

"Er — ah, It's Sunday mornin' sir. Some of da men wantsta, have a mass. So's I says sure I'll ask his highness, er — ah, I mean, the director sir, Er — ah, Can we have a mass today?"

The thought of a church service now was revolting.

Mr. Bertolucci looked hurt and blubbered out
"Blasphemy in the sight of such supreme majesty.
We viewed a woman's emotional life laid bare before us and he talks of a mass. Here in Paterson? A mass? In the church of life?"

As he spoke blazing blue tears fell from his face setting the entire scene in a spiraling motion and throwing it out in a sea of roiling flames. The blue smoke of war poured out lurking down the green hills smothering all in its wake. Blood spilled over the rocks crashing down rushing while carried down by the Passaic falls. Red water turned to falls of flowing bodies. The force swirled up spray of ever-darkening portents, disguising all the bared emotions. The only thing I could see clearly were the white bones of men falling. Longing my only emotion.
A longing to bring it all back. Just for a moment. For now though, I wait. I wait with all the others until there is enough courage among us to see the mystery again.

FOR EMMA

Sometimes Emma
just glances understanding my way
She has a knowing smirk
it says:
I see the time we have
It will be sweet
Like summer plums

Our dreams,
small seeds
grow
like Bonsais
wizened with age
Cared for with loving hands
Creating life's abundant
landscape jewels
in miniature
to be passed down
to her children,
like great paintings
with each look
we exchange

I will cry for you when you leave
she says, unspoken
with her arms
You will live on in my dreams
In my poetry, my art
my heart of hearts
We have always been together
haven't we?

Her face is time,
and as new as
the Rudbekia
we planted
sparked
by summer's
sun

OUR FATHER'S SONS

Lucas looked up into my eyes
at five.
Tears streaming
and said —

"Poppy, when I grow up and become a father
you're going to die aren't you?"

I turned with
sweet smelling fecund
autumn wind in mind.
Flooding rains rising,
smiled
and said

"Yes."

Emma Fairchild Gorman

Lucas Orion Gorman

LATE

Struggling on a cold morning's start
braving the ether start-up spray
shot down the carb.
Came in to the world two weeks late
set against a white December blizzard,
doin' a highwire walk over the void, rolling in,
a bloody red '51 custom—taillights first.
Trying to take things in retrospect, I suppose.

"Your big fins nearly killed er! Ya know."
"Which one do ya want? The mom or the kid?"
the doctor said.
Words solemnly chewed
over and over with cotton spit
in the corners of father's mouth.
Making damn sure reminder
there was proper appreciation
for the sacrifices made.

Too much weight for a small chassis
Trying to get up to speed in the first decade
Reworking the engine, filled with potential, but
blown out of the race by hormones
and guilt-clogged air filters.
Horn sqwonked and cracked.
Untied sneakers like flat tires slugged into
life in the third power plus high test testosterone.
Too late on the brake pedal.
Flyin' through that still red traffic signal,
Even today memories persist of fresh
glass break, and screeching sounds—
that smell of gasoline soaked death
in a small green British Leyland metal coffin.
Getting it on with the reaper
raises small hairs on the seat covers
and swipes clear the windshield
of fallen black mud from lavender skies.

In the lingo of ancient mechanics
dark purple moons dance
fire flies across two decades of nights.

Even now, in the quad life and six
Death's side swipe vision-gift matured,
rear view illuminated.
Much of what's sowed finally come to fruit.
The engine is tuned and running hot
Antenna taller than most
A Craig Breedlove creative energy blastin'
setting new land speed records.
Spoken in the lingo of ancient mechanics
like pure nitro through a four barrel carb
Pedal to the metal, plush interior,
and fat whitewalls hugging chrome reverse wheels
A mean chopped and channeled, red short
with scalloped flamed quarter panels.
Smokin' for a late bloomer.
Speed racin' to the finish line
Hopin' to be late again.

PATERSON

P - a - t - e - r - s - o - n
and
P - a - r - a - d- i- s- e
have symmetry
Paradise like Paterson
starts with a—P perhaps
for the Passaic
an aboriginal name
given for the brown birth scar
of a river that slogs past
If not symmetry, then at least
Constellation, certainly
for the double quaternary
of letters.
Eight, one shy of the nine muses

She is a molasses slash
The Passaic river
My spiritual Ganges,
that defines East from West
Like Hermes, like Moses,
my grandfather admonished me
for not being aware of hits
by golden skinned carp
on banks of the Passaic.
Admonished, for not seeing
the small circles form
at the end of my fishing line.
My grandfather like Moses admonished me
For asking to see the mystery
rather than be it.

The Passaic's swirling sepia
surface is mesmerizing
We drunkenly watched
the small golden mouths of sun
opened and closed on the surface
Their radiance filled the eyes
of all who could see —
Paterson's paradise,
Paterson's paradise,
Paterson's paradise —
in the slow-moving, high noon slag
the rising smell of mud.
The many colored men of the river.

Our life's connection
a thin blue filament stitched
through the eyes of a switch of bamboo
resting in the crooked crotch
of a divining y-shaped
dowsing stick.
pressed into the earth
We waited as all men do
for the black carps' call
stuck on the earth for now
casting a pale purple shadow
at the river's red edge.
We made an offering of corn
on the end of a sharp hook
tied to a length of time.

The OOOOOMmm I heard,
pass between us on that day
the topic of life's mystery.
Where is the source of the river Grandpa,
can we see it some day?"
"Just watch your pole, boy." Is all he'd say.
His wisdom passed on to me
My youth couldn't see the quiet purpose
beginning with — P

Perhaps, a talisman in the silence,
an amulet of peace, strong armor for the walk on
the razor's edge,
or out of the Passaic, his arm
raised for a cast,
the pole's an Excaliber for me.

Golden mouths of flickering sun
filled us with the epiphany of eternal love
My Grandfather and me
Trekked to Benares
at the head of the Ganges
Leapt into Arthur's journeys
Cried for Milton's loss
Burned in the noon sun.

Our life's connection
a thin blue filament stitched
through the eyes of a switch of bamboo
resting in the crooked crotch
of a divining y shaped
dowsing stick.
Forever impaled
into the heart of hearts
now pouring out
of the mouths of sons.